The Third Climber

Paul Groves

Hutchinson

London Melbourne Sydney Auckland Johannesburg

Hutchinson & Co. (Publishers) Ltd

An imprint of the Hutchinson Publishing Group

17–21 Conway Street, London W1P 6JD

Hutchinson Group (Australia) Pty Ltd
30–32 Cremorne Street, Richmond South, Victoria 3121
PO Box 151, Broadway, New South Wales 2007

Hutchinson Group (NZ) Ltd
32–34 View Road, PO Box 40–086, Glenfield, Auckland 10

Hutchinson Group (SA) (Pty) Ltd
PO Box 337, Bergvlei 2012, South Africa

First published 1977
Reprinted 1979, 1982, 1984

Printed in Great Britain at The Anchor Press
and bound by Wm Brendon & Son Ltd, both of
Tiptree, Essex.

ISBN 0 09 131601 4

1

It was hard going up the track. They had been on it now for seven days. Each day got that bit harder. Each day their backs had to bend a bit more as the slope got steeper. Each day the packs on their backs seemed heavier.

The bearers had the biggest loads. But they made light of them. They were used to living high up in the mountains. They laughed and grinned, showing their white teeth. But to someone like Bill White just out from England, this was hard going. It found out the weak spots in his body.

Every two hours they stopped. That was heaven to Bill White. He flung his pack down. As it left his back he felt as if he was floating. Floating on thin air.

He took a drink from his water bottle. The water came from a mountain stream and it tasted like cool wine. He just had to dip his bottle in the stream. Up on the mountain they would have to drink melted snow.

He looked down the valley. He could no longer see the town. He was really on his way now.

2

Was he mad to be here? Was he mad to leave the green of England for these barren mountains? He often had these thoughts at the start of a climb. He knew they would go. They would go once he got away from Base Camp. There was no time to think after that. All the time went in planning. Planning the next hour's climb. Planning where to put your hand or foot next.

They set off again. Milton was in front. Why did Milton always want to go in front? Why did he have to lead the bearers? They knew the track like the backs of their hands.

He did not like Milton. He had never understood what made him tick. Most climbers don't talk much. But Milton talked all the time. Bill could see him now, telling the Sherpas what to do. He liked giving orders. Yet even though Milton talked so much Bill did not really know him.

Why do people climb mountains? Is it the wish to get to the top? Is it to try and master a fear of heights? Is it because once you have done it mountain climbing is like a drug?

4

He was sure that this last reason was why Milton did it. You could tell by the look in his eyes. When he looked at you his deep-set eyes seemed to go through you. As though he was not looking at you, but at the mountain behind.

Bill did not like climbing with Milton. He did not like it because in a tight spot Milton would show off and take too many risks. A good climber never takes a risk unless he has to.

He was annoyed that Milton was on the climb. He thought of the good climbers back in England. Men who were longing to climb these mountains. But Milton knew how to get money for climbs. Milton had helped raise a lot of money.

Bill stopped to take a last look down the valley. Three more days of this and after that they could get up to the real stuff. Then he would be climbing with Brad Smith. He would not think about Milton then.

But he did not know then than Milton would be very much on his mind. That his whole life would be changed by Milton.

3

Bill was thinking about Milton again. It was four weeks later. They were up in Camp Four. He was with Brad Smith, Ken Conway and Milton. The plan had been for Ken and Milton to go for the summit the next day.

But Ken was ill. On the climb up from Camp Three he had said he was OK. But now he had to admit he was ill. He had a pain in his chest. Brad, who was a doctor, thought he had a bad lung. He got part of a message back to Base Camp but then the radio went dead on him. He kept trying again but he could not make contact.

And here was Milton saying that he would go alone. The silly fool was saying that he would climb to the summit on his own. He wanted Bill and Brad to take Ken back down to Camp Three.

Brad was being very cool about it, Bill thought. He told Milton that no climber could do it alone. He told him it was his duty to get Ken back to Camp Three.

Milton got angry at this. He shouted at Brad. His voice and heavy breathing filled the small tent.

He said they were trying to stop him doing the climb. He said they didn't want him to get to the top before they did.

In the end Brad told him to shut up. All this fuss was making Ken worse. He was very sick and needed sleep. Brad also said that he would make sure that Milton had a go at the summit. But not on his own.

4

Bill White knew it before he awoke. Men who are close in a tent on a mountain side can sense things. Bill knew it in that half-sleeping, half-waking state that comes before dawn. Yes, Milton had gone.

He woke Brad. Brad cursed Milton. Together they crawled out. There in the half light was Milton a hundred feet up on the rock face. They could see his orange clothes.

They shouted at him. Again and again they called. But Milton could not hear or he took no notice. He was climbing fast. They could not catch him up and stop him.

Ken Conway was worse. He was in pain all the time now. His breathing was not good. They had to get him down to Camp Three. From there the Sherpas could take him down to Base. Ken did not want to go. He said he would be all right, if he rested. But Brad said he must go. He could see how bad Ken was.

It took them eight hours to get down to Camp Three. They planned to rest there until Ken was fit to go on down. Then they could go back to Camp Four and try for the summit.

At first they were lucky. A Sherpa had come up from Base with some tablets for Ken. But within hours their luck changed. The storm clouds closed in. They were stuck in Camp Three for three days. Brad looked after Ken and waited for the storm to pass.

When at last there was a break in the clouds they looked up the mountain. Was Milton there? Was he alone in the storm? Once they thought they saw him. But they were not sure. Maybe he was back in Camp Four waiting for the storm to pass.

The storm lifted in the end. Ken Conway was a lot better now. With the help of the Sherpas he would make it back to Base.

Bill talked a lot about Milton. But Brad said he must push Milton from his mind. He must keep his mind on getting to the top, now that the weather was good.

But it was not easy to forget about Milton. Bill kept thinking about him. He could almost see his face. Almost see his eyes, with that fixed, far-away look.

5

Now this was it. It was now or never. They were on the last bit of the climb. The climb for the summit. They had left Camp Four two hours ago. The two men clung like flies to the side of the mountain. Far above them was the rocky peak.

The pack on Bill's back was heavy. As well as his oxygen supply and climbing gear he was carrying a tent. A new sort of tent. It had not yet been tested and Bill and Brad had been asked to try it out. Now Bill was sorry he had said yes. On the climb to the top there was no need for a tent. It was just an extra load to carry.

Bill stopped. He was breathing hard. His arms were tired. His legs were tired. Every part of his body was stiff. Here the rock face was like a wall. And above the climb was harder still.

Below him was a sheer drop. He looked at the rope above him. A thin bit of nylon. If the nylon rope broke, he would drop three thousand feet. He would drop onto the ice below. He could see the ice shining in the sun. It glinted like broken glass.

But up here on the rock face the sun was not shining. It was bitter cold. The wind was blowing so hard, it could blow him off the face. Then, if the rope did not hold . . . .

He told himself what a fool he was. He did not really like heights. Each time he told himself that this climb would put an end to his fear. But it did not. And still he went on climbing.

When he looked behind he could see dark clouds. The clouds were heavy with snow. He knew what that meant. Had Brad seen them as well? Would all their hopes be dashed?

At that moment Bill was leading. They took it in turns. Below him Bill could see Brad. Was Brad thinking about the big drop? Bill wished he could get it out of his mind. He had to think about getting on to the over-hang. That must take all his thoughts.

6

The over-hang was just above him. It was a ledge of rock jutting out. It stuck out about ten feet from the rock face. You had to climb under it; fix the rope; and then swing out.

Once on the over-hang he could help Brad up. Then they could rest. They could rest and have a snack. Bill could check his oxygen supply too. There was something the matter with it. Maybe a leak or a blocked pipe. That was why he was breathing so hard. That was why he was tired and his body was so slow.

To get to the summit you had to have oxygen. They were at over 20 000 feet. Bill would be annoyed if lack of oxygen stopped him. He did not mind if lack of skill stopped him. Or bad weather. That couldn't be helped. But something wrong with the oxygen supply annoyed him. It should have been checked.

He looked up at the over-hang. A climber likes to have three parts of his body on the rock face. A hand and two feet. Or two hands and one foot. Then he feels safe. But to get on the over-hang he had to swing out. Swing out over the big drop. Swing out and trust a thin nylon rope.

Bill knocked in a metal peg. The rope would be fixed to the pegs. Then he could swing out. Had he knocked it in well? Had he picked the best spot? Would it hold? These thoughts went slowly through his mind as he knocked in each peg. His brain was slow because of the lack of oxygen. This made his hands slow at knocking in the pegs. What would Brad be thinking of his slowness?

He thought of his family. They were safe back in London. They were not daft. They did not want to get to the top of the mountains. At times like this he felt like a madman. His legs were cold. His hands were stiff with cold. He could have been by a fire back in London with his family. If only he did not have this madness. This need to climb mountains. If only he did not have the fear.

He looked behind again. Yes, the snow clouds were nearer. They could be in a snow storm in ten minutes. He looked down at Brad. Brad was ten feet below. Brad was waiting for him to get on to the over-hang.

Brad was not like Bill. Brad always kept cool. He did not flap. He would not be thinking about the drop to the ice below. He would not be thinking about his family. Brad was the climber to be with in a fix.

Bill swung out. He had now fixed the ropes. They felt firm. That made him feel better. Now he could inch along under the over-hang. The ropes held him like a cradle. But you did not want to rock the cradle. That put a strain on the pegs. Yet it was difficult not to swing about. The wind was blowing up the face in great gusts.

He longed to be safe on top of the over-hang. He knew it was only a small ledge. The climbers who had reached this same spot last year had told him about it back home. They had got stuck on it and could go no higher. They stopped on this ledge. It was about two feet wide. But at least you could rest on it. He could look at the oxygen supply as well.

Ah, he had got his hands on the edge. Almost there now. He got his feet on the rope and pulled himself up. He could see over the top of the ledge. Oh, God! Oh, dear God!

7

There was a body on the ledge. It filled the two-foot wide space. It was lying neatly on the ledge. The legs were together. The arms were by its sides. It was as though it had been placed there.

He inched up so he could see the face. Yes, it was Milton. There was a crust of ice on his nose and chin. And his eyes were wide open. You would know those staring eyes anywhere. They were looking straight up. Straight up at the summit.

As far as Bill could see, Milton had not fallen. There was no sign of blood. His legs and arms did not look twisted or broken. It was as though Milton had just gone to sleep. That was if you did not look at the staring eyes.

In his left hand Milton was holding a flag. The flag he wanted to put on the summit. So Milton had not made it. He had died 300 feet from the top. Bill felt sorry he had not made it. To die for nothing. That was bad luck.

But the body gave Bill another problem. How could he get onto the ledge? There was no room. Milton was in the way. He would have to get the body off the ledge. Maybe he could rope it to the over-hang. Then they could have a go at getting it down when they came back.

He waved down to Brad. But Brad did not understand the signal. He just waved back and went on climbing.

Slowly Bill climbed onto Milton's body. He gripped a leg with one hand and a boot with the other. Then he pulled himself up. He knew the body must have been there some time, but the hardness surprised him. The body was ice-hard. And it was frozen solid to the ledge.

He picked around it with his ice axe. But his oxygen supply was worse. It was like lifting a heavy hammer. He could not shift the body on his own. He would need Brad's help. There would just be room for the two of them, if they stood on top of the body.

Bill looked over the edge but he could not see Brad. He must be swinging out under the over-hang. He would just have to wait till Brad's hands gripped the edge. He just hoped that would not be too long. He pulled in the rope a bit.

The snow clouds were now almost on them. They

would have to get the body off. It looked as though
they would have to pitch the tent on the ledge. If the
weather closed in, they could not go for the summit.
And it might take hours to fix the oxygen in such a
spot.

Although the rope joined Bill to Brad, for a moment
he felt alone in space. Then he saw the eyes of Milton
again. He put his hand over them.

8

Brad's hands gripped the ledge. Bill helped him till Brad's face was level with the body. 'It's Milton!' shouted Bill. Brad pulled himself up onto the body.

Brad sat down and slowly took off his mask. 'I can't shift him,' said Bill, 'and I'm not getting any oxygen.' 'Let me have a go,' said Brad.

They chipped away at the ice for ten minutes. But it did not do much good. They just got Milton's head free and one foot. The snow clouds were right over them now. The first flakes were falling. They looked at each other. 'It's lucky we've got the tent,' said Brad. 'We'll have to put it up and sort out your oxygen.' Bill nodded. 'Let's hope the tent is OK,' he said. 'It hasn't been tested yet.'

The plan was to pitch the tent just above Milton. It was made to fit onto almost a sheer rock face. It would take a little time getting in the metal pegs.

But the weather took a sudden turn. The wind started blowing more strongly than ever. The snow flakes came down like a sheet. And the cold air bit into them. If they wanted to stay alive they had to put the tent up quickly.

They did not say anything but they knew they must fix the base of the tent to Milton's body. They could use the foot they had freed at one end and the head at the other. It was very difficult. They wished they could take their gloves off but this would be madness.

Bill was at the head end. He felt better when Milton's face was covered with the base of the tent. He had not done quite such a good job as Brad. But it would do.

Bill had been in many tight spots. There had been that time in Scotland. He had broken his leg. Brad had made a hole for them in the snow for the night. Luckily the rescue team had found them in the morning.

Then there was the time in the Alps. They were on a rock face like this. A storm had blown up, and lightning struck all round them. They were lit up like a pin-ball machine. That was the time he felt closest to death.

But there had been nothing like this: 20 000 feet up in a blizzard. Sitting on a dead man in a tiny tent.

But neither of them said anything about it.

9

'Let's see what's up with your oxygen supply,' said Brad. 'I think it's a valve,' said Bill. They spent an hour fiddling with it. Now that Bill was sitting out resting he could breathe with his mask off. They could not see what was wrong with it. It should have worked.

'Let's eat,' said Brad, 'and have another look later.' Bill was not hungry any more. But his throat was dry from his quick breathing. He badly needed a drink.

They got the stove going. It was standing just about on Milton's chest, Bill thought. He reached out to get some snow and ice for the drink. He forgot to put on his top glove. He cursed himself. They had enough problems without frost-bite. It took him half an hour of blowing and rubbing to get his hand back to life.

They ate their food in silence. It was a relief not to have to shout against the wind. Then it dropped a bit Bill wanted to talk. He needed to take his mind off Milton. He couldn't forget that he was sitting on a dead man's body. 'A penny for your thoughts,' he said.

'It's all ifs,' said Brad. 'If we can get your oxygen

going and if the storm breaks, then we can have a go at the summit tomorrow. We have food for another day. Then we will have to go down.' He did not add: 'If the weather will let us get down.'

'What about Milton?' asked Bill. 'That's another if,' said Brad. 'If we can get him down, we will. If not, God rest his soul.'

A clap of thunder came from down the valley. The wind got up again.

10

All through the afternoon the storm raged. At times there would be a lull. Then Brad would look out. But down in the valley there were more snow clouds. Things looked grim. In these mountains, storms went on for days.

It was a bad time of the year to climb. This time was always a risk. Bill thought of the meeting back home. They had been given the chance to come because a French team had dropped out. They knew it was not the best time.

Milton had really made them come. Bill could see him at the meeting now. No one had ever got to the summit by going up the east face. Milton had said that the British must do it. He had talked on and on. Bill could see his eyes now. His head was tilted. Milton always looked up.

Bill was having no more luck with the oxygen supply. He had stripped it down. All the parts looked OK. But it still did not work well.

Why couldn't he shut Milton out of his mind? He was sure Brad had. Brad looked so calm. He had spent the afternoon checking the rope and planning the way they would climb to the summit. He had hoped to see it from here. There was only three hundred feet to go. But the summit was always in cloud.

The light began to fade. They must settle down for the long night. But first they must have a meal. Bill got the stove going again. They could not leave it on to warm up the tent. The didn't have enough fuel.

Bill liked getting the meals. It was then he felt most calm on a mountain. At least it would take his mind off Milton. 'I'll have roast duck,' said Brad. He grinned. Brad was normally full of fun. But this was the first joke they had had all day. 'Yes, sir,' said Bill. 'And how would you like your wine? Chilled, sir?' Brad grinned again. He had a big wide smile. Bill put the beef cubes in the pot.

They ate their meal slowly, as climbers do. Meal times are a time for talk. Past climbs. Climbs still to be done. That was the odd thing about Milton. He had rushed his food. He rushed it as though he could not spare the time to eat.

Now Bill was thinking about Milton again. He could eat no more. Damn it, he was sitting on Milton's face.

Brad was talking about the way to the summit now. He had some photos shot from a plane. If the weather would only get better they could make it. All the talk now was about getting to the top. Not a word was said about getting Milton down.

By the time they had looked at the photos it was getting very dark. They must get some sleep. The wind still howled round the tent.

It was very cold. Bill had known cold on many climbs. But never cold like this. Cold that got inside the tent. Cold that got inside the clothes. Cold that dug into the bones. They could not stamp their feet or swing their arms. Was it just himself? Was he ill? 'Are you cold?' he asked Brad. 'It's a bit nippy,' said Brad. Bill knew then that Brad was feeling it as well. He felt a bit better.

Bill could not relax. He knew he was sitting on Milton's face. He could feel the nose. He shifted to get on top of the chest. This pushed him right against Brad. But he might get warm that way.

Brad was soon asleep. He was OK. He could sleep on a clothes line. But Bill was still wide awake. How would he fill his mind? How would he fill the long hours of the night?

11

But he did sleep. He slept for about an hour. He dreamt he was in a big city. There were tall buildings all round. He was trying to cross a road. On the other side were his wife and children. But he could not cross because of the traffic. He was afraid his children might run across to him. It was a dream he often had when he was away.

He woke up and felt drops of sweat on his face. Yes, he was surprised to find himself sweating. The tent was much warmer. Brad was still sleeping deeply. He could hear his deep breathing. He tried to shift himself without waking Brad.

The dream had now gone from his mind. He was fully awake. He was not sweating now but it was warmer in the tent. Perhaps this meant better weather. The wind was still blowing. Perhaps it was a warmer wind?

Then he had a thought. Was there any chance that the heat of their bodies would melt the ice? Could they melt the ice that gripped Milton's body to the ledge? If that happened would they fall into space? The base of the tent was fixed to Milton's body.

Would the pegs on the rock face hold? They could fall into the night.

No, he was being silly. He could not be fully awake. The ice would not melt. Not so high up the mountain.

He dozed off. Woke. Dozed again. Woke again. Each time he could hear Brad's heavy breathing. Yes, Brad was sleeping well. Bill wished it was him. He could feel the rise and fall of Brad's body.

Breathe in. Breathe out. Breathe in. Breathe out. Breathe in. Breathe in. Breathe out. Breathe out. There was something funny about Brad's breathing. It sounded as if there were two men breathing. It sounded as if there were two men as well as himself in the tent! Two men!

He was now fully awake. This was no dream. There were two men breathing as well as himself in the tent. He put his hand on Milton's body. Had it come back to life? He felt to see if the chest rose and fell. No, it didn't. What a fool he was. Was he going mad?

He felt for his torch. He found it and pressed the switch. Yet he was afraid of what he might see.

He flashed the torch round the small tent. No! He

rubbed his eyes. He could see a big bulge in the tent wall. He and Brad had their backs to the rock wall. The tent bulged out on the other side where it should have been blown in by the wind. It was from this bulge that the sound of breathing came.

Bill White had known fear on the mountains. Any climber who is honest will tell of fear. But Bill had never panicked. Not until now. Now he felt he must rip open the tent. Rip open the wall of the tent and leap down the rock face. Away from this thing that breathed in the tent. He gripped his knife.

But a picture of his wife and children went through his mind. His little girl crying. Big tears in her eyes. This thought saved him. He took his hand off his knife.

After what seemed an age he got his hand on Brad's arm. He shook him. 'For God's sake, Brad, wake up!' 'What is it?' Brad did not open his eyes. 'For God's sake, Brad, is there something in this tent or am I mad?' 'It's the lack of oxygen,' said Brad still half asleep. 'For God's sake, Brad. Brad! Stop breathing and listen!'

Brad came to. He looked at the bulge in the tent lit by the torch in Bill's shaking hand. He held his breath and listened to the strange breathing. 'You're right,' he said. 'You're not mad.' He took his pipe out of his pocket.

'Don't you ever panic?' shouted Bill. 'God, we must get out of here.' 'It's death out of here in the dark,' said Brad. 'And you know it. Whatever is with us in the tent cannot harm us. Not if we keep our minds calm. If it is evil, it can only harm the mind. Not the body.'

Brad began to talk. He talked about climbing. Bill noticed that if Brad was talking, the breathing became quiet. If he stopped it became heavy again. He said a few words himself. It helped. His heart slowed. Perhaps he could get through the night.

Dawn came up. They still talked. The two of them. Just as if they were alone in the tent. Then suddenly Brad yelled: 'The wind! It's stopped.' He put his head out. 'It's stopped snowing. I can see the sun! Let's look at your oxygen supply again.'

'I'll try it once more,' said Bill. He did. He turned it on full. 'It's working!' he yelled. 'We can go for the summit!'

As he said this, the breathing of the thing stopped. The bulge in the tent went as well. They looked at each other and grinned. 'The summit!' they yelled.

12

It was three hundred feet to the top. They would have to get up quickly. And then back down again to Camp Four. They had to hurry. The weather might change. In any case they had to get back before dark. The going should not be as bad as below the over-hang. But when you were this high any climbing was tricky. A hand or a foot could slip and . . . .

It should have been easier than under the over-hang but it was not. Brad led. The rock was not too steep and sloped up to where he could see the summit. But as they climbed, the summit seemed to get no nearer. Cracks were hard to find for the hands. Ice steps had to be cut much of the way. The sun was shining and the wind had dropped. It should have been easy. Brad had an odd feeling too. As though some force was holding him back. Trying to stop him getting to the summit.

Below him Bill had a feeling there was another climber on the rope. A third climber. Someone out to the right of Brad. The rope still looked OK. Yet there was this feeling.

Brad had to keep pushing himself. Once his foot

slipped on an ice step as though it had been pulled out. They were in a hurry. But he would have to take more care.

They stuck to their task. It was the hardest climb they had ever done. But suddenly the ground fell away on all sides. Brad was ten feet from the top. He had never seen a view like this before. He grinned down to Bill and helped him up. They hurried and stumbled the last few steps to the top.

They stood there on the summit, grinning and waving their arms. They had made it. At first they did not see the Union Jack.

But there in the snow was Milton's flag. They knew it was his. The flag they had last seen in Milton's hand was here on the top of the mountain.

They said nothing. But a look passed between them that said everything. Had Milton made it to the summit and died on the way down? Did he have two flags? Or had there been a third climber with them that morning? A climber who had just got to the top before them.

They placed their flag by Milton's. They looked at the flags side by side. Took the photos. And then turned to go down the mountain. Bill could not wait to get back to the over-hang. He wanted to see if the flag was still in Milton's hand.

They went back the way they had come. It was easier going down than coming up. This time Bill went first. Brad followed. It was still a long way to the ledge but they kept looking out for Milton's body. It would not be easy to see in all this ice and snow. But they would see the tent. That would help them find the spot.

As they plodded on, grey clouds began to gather in the sky. They would have to hurry. Where was the tent? They must see it soon. Maybe they were going the wrong way. No. This was right. There were the steps cut in the ice.

Suddenly there was a great flash of lightning. The mountain seemed to shake. Bill started to slip. He must have slid down ten feet. Then he felt the pull on the rope. Brad had held him. He was safe.

Feeling a bit sick with shock he sat down. He looked down. Then he had another look. There was no tent. No body. No ledge. The whole over-hang had gone. It had broken off from the rock face. And it had taken Milton's body with it.

Brad came down to join him. They looked down on to the ice below. They could see nothing. Just a white blanket of new snow. Milton had gone. There would be no time to look for the body. Another storm was closing in. They would have to get down.

Now they would never know about the flag. Milton would have to stay there. Below the mountain he had climbed.